THE GREAT INDOORS

THE GREAT INDOORS

poems by

TERENCE WINCH

Story Line Press
Brownsville, Oregon

Acknowledgments:
Adrift, Aerial, American Poetry Review, Barney, The Brooklyn Review, City Paper, Hanging Loose, Hard Press, Mag City, St. Mark's Poetry Project Newsletter, Shiny, Transfer, Venice, The Washington Review, ZZZZZ. Some of these poems also appeared in *American Poetry Since 1970: Up Late*, ed. Andrei Codrescu; *Out of This World: An Anthology of the St. Mark's Poetry Project 1966–1991*, ed. Anne Waldman; and *Hang Together: The Hanging Loose Press 20th Anniversary Anthology*.

The author wishes to thank the National Endowment for the Arts and the D.C. Commission on the Arts and Humanities for generous grants that helped provide support and encouragement.

Story Line Press thanks the National Endowment for the Arts, the Nicholas Roerich Museum, The Andrew W. Mellon Foundation, and our individual contributors.

First American printing

Book design and cover photograph (*Number* 9, 1993)
by Susan Campbell

Library of Congress Cataloging-in-Publication Data

Winch, Terence.
The great indoors : poems / by Terence Winch
p. cm.
ISBN 0-934257-89-2 (pbk.)
I. Title
PS3573.14789G7 1994
811'.54—dc20 94-41989
CIP

Published by Story Line Press, Inc.
Three Oaks Farm, Brownsville, Oregon 97327

for Susan and Michael

CONTENTS

1. City of Pleasure

Civilized Atmospheres 18
My Friends 22
In the Milky Light 24
Blue Boy 25
The Rules of the Game 26
Watching It Rain on Television 27
Split Image 28
Black Market 29
The Fabulous Evening 30
Iron Eyes 32
The Starry Wilderness 33
Arousal 34
Takoma Park Metro 35
In a Beautiful Car, through the Lovely Streets 36
Long Distance 38
Bad Influence 39
Surfaces 40
The Bells Are Ringing for Me and Chagall 41
The Summer in Space 42
Swamp 43

A Pair of Aces 44
Third World of the Mind 45
Comfortable Strangers 46
Tactics 47
Suburb of Drunk Actresses 48
Success Story 49

II. *Burning in Rush Hour*

The Drift of Things 52
Fiesta 54
Passage 55
The Riot Act 56
A Few Words about Myself 58
Taking a Turn for the Worse 60
Tripping up the Stairs 62
Living Legend 63
Applause 64
Fugitive 65
The Them Decade 66
Influencing the Past 68
Naked Walls 69

III. WHAT THE FLATNESS CONTAINS

Mysteries 72

I Hate Ethiopian Music 74

Lapse of Luxury 75

The Nihilists Have Nothing to Worry About 76

The Clean Sweep of the Stars 77

The Club Scene 79

Memorial Day 81

Hamburger Gardens 82

The Moon 83

White Reflections 84

Jewels 85

The Love You Take 86

On the Beach 87

My Emotions 88

Some Waves 89

Religious Articles 90

The Dreamers by the Fountain 92

Destiny 94

The White Magic of Decay 95

IV. A DREAM OF HALF CIRCLES

Ghosts 98

Les Hommes d'Aujourd'Hui 99

A Piece of the Action 100

The Rebirth of Traffic 102

Ashes 104

Cracks 105

Certain Things Happened 106

Amnesia 108

city of pleasure

Civilized atmospheres

The bar is filled with a foul odor, something

to do with the sewage system. People don't mind

one bit. They smoke, talk, make time, drink, dance.

We don't mind either. We like to see people having fun.

We think there should be more fun in all our lives.

And more sex and money. We want everyone to have

more power, as much power as they would like,

because we know how important power is to people.

We want everyone we know to be the boss on the job

and at home too. We want them to get what they want

because when they do, they're happy and we're happy.

We want them to have bigger and better houses and apartments.

More beautiful lovers. We want them to have lean, hard

bodies and perfect cardiovascular health.

We want their health clubs to be radiant and spotless.

We'd like to see their children turn out radiant too.

It is threatening to rain. We hate rain. We hate even more
the heavy oppressive atmosphere that precedes rain. We hate
the bad smell in the bar and we don't like the people in the bar
because they seem so pompous. Their breath is horrible
and they have pot bellies and their clothing stinks of cigarettes.
It is getting dark two hours before it should. That really makes
us mad and depresses us too. Darkness. We hate darkness
because it is so scary.

Nobody calls us anymore, so we call them
because we don't want to be left alone up here
in the dark with no one to talk to. But there's no
answer, or we get the answering machine and leave
a message, or they are there but they just can't
talk to us right now because they're too busy, or even worse,
they're expecting a more important call than ours.

It's pouring now. Thunderous skies are opening up.
Everything is wet. We hate to get wet.
We closed the windows just in time, but now

it's airless in here and we can't breathe.

We don't like work. The coming and going,
the politics, the give and take.
We can live without it. The mindless routine
day after day: the bus, the coffee break, the paperwork.

We don't want anyone to have to go to work
with those disgusting bad-smelling people
who think they're so important. Don't they know
that no one is indispensable? What about when you die?
Do they ever think of that?

We don't want to have to come home from work
in the scary wet darkness and then have to leave again
for the smelly bar where those absolutely horrible people
drink their drinks. We don't want anyone
we know to have to do it either.

We'd like everyone to stay home where it's dry and peaceful,
where they can watch movies and eat whatever they want,

sleeping in a chair, listening to the sound of a car horn,

the scary wet darkness enveloping them in its dream.

My friends

for Doug Lang

They came here first in a car shaped like a heart

and now they depart as brilliant jazz musicians.

They arrived in full costume, rolling north

through a winter of neon.

Now I watch them leaving me

in a moonlight of falsettos.

They are singing goodbye to me in the echo chamber

and I am smiling at them from my king-size window.

You get the idea.

I was always making way for the others.

Now, like an intake of breath, I am beside myself.

They tell me that God is inside us and I tell them

our fathers' teeth were white with fear. The streets

that I used to see from my window have faded away.

The birds I used to hear in the trees have fallen

on evil days. The beautiful girls who used to wear skintight

silver foil now dress in ugly shoes with big square tongues.

And the immaculate boys in their red velour are the old men

who rock their bodies back and forth in grief.

But I take comfort in a dreamlike kind of consciousness

in which every breath is like my last breath

and all my friends are quiet as brides

skirting along on sheets of ice.

IN THE MILKY LIGHT

for Robert Slater

I came out of the skies into the capital.

Snow covered the parked Volkswagens.
They were like huge white stones.

"There is an erotic smell in the automobile,"
I told my friend in Kansas City.

He said crazy things I didn't catch.

We both looked up.
The jets were barely visible in the hundred-degree
haze that befouled the mysterious sky.
I felt an intense craving for simplicity.

The women in white talk their dreamy white-love talk.
I am watching that empty corner, keeping my hands
on the table. Another woman glides through the landscape.
We actually live here. We're laughing. There are lots
of "ooohs" and "aaahs."

I want to go somewhere for sex and music, somewhere
inexhaustible. I want to live! My blood rushes,
my legs swing up and down, my arms are wrapped around me.

Blue boy

Suddenly, I'm not half the man I used to be.
Somebody has been watching me and making me say
incredibly dumb things. For example, whenever anyone
says anything to me, I repeat it back to them as a question.
If someone says to me, "I just came back from the supermarket
with a loaf of bread," I say, "You just came back
from the supermarket with a loaf of bread?"

That man is here. He is a horrible blue color.
He doesn't like me and I don't like him.
He wants to make me this horrible blue color too.
All the people are blue here.
Blue boys, blue girls. A deep Riviera blue.
I feel it going up my legs down my arms
this horrible blue color.

They say to me,"Why don't you get lost?"
I say stupidly, "Why don't I get lost?"
They look at me with contempt.
"That's what we said," they say.
I am almost about to say
"That's what you said?"
but I catch myself in time.

I travel constantly now,
trying to make the transition
from a successful emotional life to a life
of misery in which all
my ambitions are fulfilled.

THE RULES OF THE GAME

I awoke suddenly, thinking someone

was in the room with me, sitting

right over there in the easy chair.

I stood in the grass next to my food

as the red paint faded from my body.

I pressed another button and the birds

started singing in their cages. In the milky

light I could see the waitresses leaving

and the policemen giggling in their squad cars.

I was dizzy and had no money. He said he heard

my call. I lost control of my feet and started

to dream of touching shoulders with you

as the oncoming traffic rushed towards us.

Watching It Rain on Television

She was sad. "What kind of place is this?" she asked.

My eyes wouldn't focus. I squatted close to the fire

and ran my hand along her feathers. They allow me

to make one phone call. She is an echo shimmering

through the traffic of head-on gestures. I am a blueprint

of pleasure absorbing desire till my brain turns black.

I confess. I get impatient. I complain.

So she stands in the room with her legs up.

I can't hold anything. When she shifts,

I shatter into a hundred different pieces

of dialogue, calling to her through a desert

in the radioactive dark.

Split image

As she reached him across the empty highlights
of sand, he nodded toward the hair on his chest
moving in the wind. They wiped the translucent
sediment from their Buicks. In his recollection
something white remained, yet it was hard
to believe the city was still there all around them.

He liked to follow the specks of amber.
"They say Dad," she said, "like their Dad was the only Dad."
He said "thank you" with the sound of the ocean breaking
out of the darkness. No music came.
She went in and turned the radio on, opened a window.
"My heart is going too fast," he said.
She raised her legs to the shore lights
so they could hear the surf through the low cement wall.

Black market

She stood on the table and clung to my fingers.

Her body seemed extraordinary to me, so intensely

alive. "Everybody dreams," I told her.

"I look into the mirror with my eyes closed," she said.

I was afraid of nothing. Her lips were parted.

I could smell her through the door. I lit a cigarette

and waved to her. She backed away from the window.

"So where is this new creature?" I asked.

I could see the Capitol building in the moonlight

and the shadows of the White House on the yellow street.

There was a smell of chalk dust in the room

as I bent over and inhaled her private alarm.

THE FABULOUS EVENING

for Liam Rector

The end of the afternoon was splendid.

Women sat at tiny pianos in the lobby

while the men showered, dressed, and bit

their lips. He said he hadn't been drinking.

She said she didn't care. She just wanted to leave.

He kissed her and she said she had something

to tell him. They found a nice cool place

to sit near the glass cage in the parking lot.

Dawn came up over the hot asphalt where the policemen

wrote their names in sand on each other's stomachs.

She could not get the roads straightened out

in her mind. The fierce, greedy day was in motion.

She didn't know what to wear and wept when she woke up

and found herself alone in the room. When he returned

he pointed to the window and told her to listen.

The far-off sound of the waves ridiculed them.

He begged her not to tell on him and she leaned
against the car and blew the smoke out in a long
white column. He stood staring at the back
of the mountain while she swaggered towards him
as the rain beat down on the tin roof. She opened
her eyes and ran her tongue across her perfect teeth.

IRON EYES

You want my fingers spread

my legs pumping, my heart jumping

lying pretty on your bed

I wept thinking of you

I slept dreaming of you

C'mere, you said, get in my car

I was your automatic pilot

My veins popped out & I became

concise & now I'm thirty-eight

and I just want to stay sober

I held your head & kissed your eyes

in the oblique black & white

age of small denials

Okay, you said, c'mon

dominate the night for me

The Starry Wilderness

I turn the lights out and look at my arms.
I am a wreck. I wish I were in Katmandu
riding in a taxi with my head against the inside
of your knee. It is airless and my bones
feel like metal.

In the hotel you said you didn't care
to imagine the face of the earth
or the golden city of pleasure. I waited
for you forever in the shallow water.

I saw you do that, you said. You told me
you had no money and I remembered
feeling the chill of the city through my wet clothes
as we watched the sun shift gears over the terminal.

AROUSAL

It was a hot and humid afternoon. I was already
unzipping my shorts when I felt those cold eyes sweep over me.
Just as the glass left my lips, my head was laid back.
Suddenly, I was the prisoner. As I returned to her mouth,
I thought she'd forgotten how to talk. I did
everything she said. My head was spinning.
I leaned forward for another glass. I staggered in
and flopped on the bed. She asked me what
I wanted. I jerked my head up to see her fiancé
kneeling on the bed. I watched her tongue and mouth
form each word. A large, fresh towel was wrapped
around me. I sank into the carpet.
Her eyes lit up. I asked her what it was
she didn't want me to make her do.

TAKOMA PARK METRO

I taste the snow on your elbows.
I love your Russian eyebrows.
I want you to play the piano, now!
My musicians sit on the curb
by the 7-11. A dark figure
strolls by under the street lamp.
A woman runs away from me
but I sit down and smoke.
The telephone stinks of perfume.
It is dusk. The red van
rattles into the parking lot.
I have no credit cards.
I can still win it in the waning seconds:
It is a luxury to draw the breath of life.

In a beautiful car, through the lovely streets

at night in the nightclub
smoke rises in the yellow spotlight
ice cubes tinkle in the crystal glasses
a saxophone is playing
'come rain or come shine'
a woman smiles at a man
lights a cigarette
tastes her drink
checks her watch

I start with my feet
get up, go about my business
I create an image of my body
then I follow my body's instructions
I imagine slight movements in my bones
(like seeing two different bodies)
my body redesigns me
I make my body more vivid

her heart pumps she transforms the way
she looks and feels he lies on the floor
on a towel she moves just out of reach
and offers to withdraw

their sexiness is a
hot philosophy
of airplane love

in the waiting room
the next day, Americans crowd around
while pretty young women part
the green shower curtain

and step out naked one by one,
fat red towels in hand

Long distance

You can hear the emotional half-life
of ex-lovers by holding a dead
telephone to your ear, the old
sweet talk, the horrible fights
of long ago in sidewalk cafes
connected into your brain again
on this, the birthday of the Marquis
de Sade, June 2nd. High noon.
I am alone in my room watching
the day (overcast, heavy) trying
to lift itself into the sky.
I can't get anything done today.
I picture myself as an old man in a chair:
white hands, white teeth, white hair.

Bad influence

I knew she was a little crazy, so I decided

to follow her. I was always a fool.

At three a.m. she called a taxi & told them

to send a cab to the back of the restaurant.

When she got home, she told the driver to

wait until she was safely in her building.

Once in her apartment, she called her mother's

number & hung up after one ring. Then she

doubled back to my place & stuck a note

in my door knocker. The note read: 'Can we

get together & talk about this as soon as possible?'

She asked me what I wanted. I said, 'everything.'

I was drinking Boomers. I asked the bartender

what was in them. He said, 'everything.'

Surfaces

I enter with a blank look on my face,
take my clothes off and get on the table.
The room is stripped bare.
I crack my knuckles. My stomach
makes mournful noises.

I want to sleep. I pretend we are at the beach
and the breeze from the ocean blows on us.
I don't touch you. I am afraid.
I dream all night about fucking.

I keep stalling. First I can't leave the kitchen,
then I'm stuck in the living room. I can't get
out of bed. I can't get off the phone.

My heart trembles today. I consider
Louis Armstrong as a possible cure.
Sorry, honey, that I'm not much fun.
I'm better looking and richer than ever,
but these days I feel exhausted
and crazy, like Los Angeles.

THE BELLS ARE RINGING FOR ME AND CHAGALL

If you are involved in a fantasy relationship with someone
in which the sex is so good it's like a fantasy
and things happen between you that are
incredibly private and unmentionable that
you could never do with anyone else ever again
so much so that you moan with pleasure in bed and can't
believe it's really happening and don't even
bother fantasizing about anyone else or any
situation other than the one you're in, then you
are in very very serious trouble and good luck
to you. It won't last and when it ends, you'll
walk the floor and wear out your shoes.

If, on the other hand, you are involved with someone
with whom you have regular, decent sex
that feels good and normal, but that you
would never think about for a moment
when masturbating—which is by no means to put
it down—then the chances of *this* relationship lasting
a very long time, of the two of you growing old together,
are very good. But often this is simply not enough.
Or it *is* enough when what is wanted, unfortunately
or not, is more than enough.

THE SUMMER IN SPACE

for Bernard Welt

A horrible woman went out one day to walk
her dogs. I crouched over a tape recorder.
I was in a horrible mood because the horrible
red-faced man with the cigarette was selling flowers
again on the corner. I sat in my hotel room
and every couple of days, I had a horrible lunch
downtown. I could never hold still for more
than a moment. A sexy blonde in a white bikini
was leaning on a white beach chair. I paced anxiously
in the control booth. Dinner was absolutely horrible.
There is a woman, somewhere, holding up a Bulova clock
and smiling at me. I was sure of that.
Afterwards, sadly, the ice melted. And now I have to go
out into the horrible night and do horrible things.

Swamp

I get dressed, put the tape recorder on,
put the wash in the machine
& take a walk on Connecticut Avenue.
I remember the way it used to be
in 1975, before I painted my apartment,
before you left Washington for New York
in a butter-colored U-Haul
& a blue pants suit.
The helicopters chop the air
over the Hilton on the edge
of the Dupont Circle valley
where Ronald Reagan was shot.
I can't stop sweating in the laundry room.
I imagine myself at the end of August
as a little puddle in the middle
of my living room floor.
I tell my friends I am not smiling.
What you see are gas pains.
Nothing changes in my life.
I want to sleep more but I can't.
I stay awake at night like the trees,
a mild breeze blowing through
my hair in the moonlight.

A PAIR OF ACES

He jumped into the pool and came walking over to me.
I was sitting at my desk, reading the newspaper.
Just then the front doorbell rang and I felt
like my knees were going to buckle as I relaxed

my hand and opened my eyes. She reached up
and unbuttoned my shirt. The water covered me
up to my neck. I managed to ask if they
were planning to do any more work on the patio.

I said that I would be available at any time.
"Great," she said. I could hardly breathe.
I stood in the shallow end of the pool, not knowing
what to expect. I realized my helplessness.

Her eyes lit up. I relaxed my eyes and opened
my hand. He said, "What I believe is what I say."

Third World of the Mind

Each night a tide of invisible changes
floods my memory of you & I wake up
with your taste on my lips, then I eat
salt & lick the menthol off your mouth,
washing down the milk of your body
with cups of coffee & ice water
& standing in the sun on P Street
I breathe in & breathe out & soon
I forget it's 4:27 on June eleven
& I am wearing corduroy pants, blue
tee shirt, running shoes & shades
& thinking of you with a knot in my stomach.
Your refusals make me melodramatic.
Your departures hypnotize me.

Comfortable Strangers

for Cesar Vallejo

In the morning I didn't know
what had happened. Things
seemed blurry to me and I felt
funny. She smiled.

Clothes hurt my skin.
I found it hard to think about abstractions.
I washed my eyes out.

I emptied you while
you slept, she said.
I know how to do it.
She was trying to scare me.

You're beautiful, I said.
Fuck you, she told me.
At breakfast I read the paper.
Everything tastes like licorice.

I enjoy being in the world,
but all I can think about is distance.
She sleeps next to me naked
in the dark, cool bedroom.

She tastes like licorice
and I like to go down on her.
I don't want to go to work today.
My clothes ache with emptiness.

Tactics

The baby cried by the jukebox.
I went to the lobby & stared out
at the thoroughfare & waited
for quitting time. Everyone thinks
I like it here, especially you.
When actually I go crazy. I eat
all the time now.

I hear a noise
coming from the living room.
Where the cold light of the dark
on our faces wakes us.
No matter what time
this love burns our bodies
it always feels like night.

Fading shadows move through
the house. Dinner is ready.
I have been too vertical
in this life, too unlovely.

Suburb of Drunk Actresses

I hear sirens in the distance.

I see three cop cars in front of the Chateau.

I am above it all. I watch

baseball on t.v. (Yankees 3, Dodgers 0)

and complain about my cold.

Cab drivers are discovering Jesus.

So are high school kids on the Metro.

People on bicycles are wired to tiny stereos.

Pocket-sized televisions are in style.

All this is a sign of fear:

Machines shrink in direct proportion

to the growth of public anxiety (Winch's Law).

And then there you are, in black skirt and high heels,

beautiful, remote, completely lacking in self-pity.

Success story

My clothes are perfectly contoured
to my body. My shoes & socks
fit just right. My cat is a delightful
intelligent animal. My apartment
is great. The right location,
cheap rent. I eat the best food.
My friends love me. I adore them.
My lover is terrific & beautiful.
The sun is shining. There are trees
even in the slums in Washington.
I have tons of money & a gorgeous
air conditioner. Great art hangs
on my wall. I live a spine-tingling life
of delirious sex & intense happiness.

burning in rush hour

THE DRIFT OF THINGS

My darling, I said, let me rest
upon the white clouds, let me lay
my head upon the brows I think I see
in the distance, where men and women
open like wallets and the walls
rise up like walls. Where doors
slam shut like doors. Where I feel
like I feel. Where you are you.

Please talk to me across the table
in the restaurant. You say
I am wonderful as I stare
out the window thinking of
a forest where the green of the trees
looks poured on. Where I imagine
a perfect life somewhere,
my skin awash in blue ultraviolet
light, my body suspended in a tank
of harmless white ingredients. Where
my breath sweetens the air. Where
everywhere I look eyeballs are white
as eggs, white as white paint,
white as white walls
in a white room.

Somewhere, off in another room,
where I am not right now,
where I am absent,
somewhere where people who are
looking for me
won't find me,
somewhere there I sense
that it is darker and warmer

than here and that a television is on and a program
I want to watch is on the television and the people
there all love me

and they are like animals, watching me
as the headlights flash through the bathroom window,
casting an ice-blue light across the room.

FIESTA

for Beth Joselow

These landscapes are not in my mind

while I drive my vermillion car

through the columns of white flame.

I am so drunk right now that the forest

seems to whistle over my head:

These work fields. This desert of faces.

I have re-decorated

my ghostly city crash by crash.

Where the Washington Monument once stood

there is now only a rust-colored clock

ticking above a cluster of unpainted buildings.

Where Lincoln lived is now a car skeleton

parked on a street of hands,

a jungle of meters. Where Lincoln died,

so did we all die in a small room

on a short bed, generals and family

members whispering out of earshot.

Passage

The bus is on fire but the passengers

do not mind. They close the windows.

They watch the leaves quivering on the trees.

It is dusk. There is nothing so sexy, so convivial,

as a bus ride in the morning, the caffeine rushing

through our blood streams. But that is not the way

it is right now. Now people are tired. They smell bad.

They will never have sex again. That is all behind

them now. They stare out the window. The day is over.

We glide over bridges past lovely parks.

How we would like to have a dog,

and to be young again, and high on drugs, and out of work

with no memory of buses burning in rush hour,

the office door smashing into the file cabinet,

our colleagues weeping in the corridor.

THE RIOT ACT

for Michael Lally

I walked into this room
the one we're in right now
where I knew some friends
of mine would be hanging out
I heard a piano playing
It was a cool April night
I sipped my coffee & felt deranged
Something was going down
the tubes again
I live in a cube in Washington
DC It's part of my contract

The boss comes in He's fat
and lazy and makes us listen
to C&W songs The assistant boss
is dressed in black leotards
We talk about Ralph Lauren
and Calvin Klein   I blow dry
the tree in front of my building

I take the subway to the office I take
a cab to the bus stop I ride the bus
home I check the mail I come home
open the door I watch t.v.

I am alone in the world time zone
There are people here but they are eating
and getting fat A beautiful woman stares
at her feet Doctors sit under the trees
discussing good places to cry

When I arrived at the office
I started to feel redeemed

perhaps because the most resonant objects—
inhalers, coffee tables, ice buckets—
were spread out before me
in a clutter of violent emotion
that I felt somehow concluded me

I was still unreleased
The day is full of eyes
The hallways are elbows, knuckles, knees
I xerox my memo
Men are spitting and clearing their throats
I check the language over and over:
is it okay? are the dates real?

I am sick of the world of material things
I am frightened
Do not take my blood please, Doctor
From tonight on, I will live
like a Franciscan
eating what the pigs won't eat
talking to the fish, the birds
wondering what it's really like in Santa Cruz
filled with the love of God

But today right now I live with my enemies
in age-ravaged unspoken love
in an immense building downtown
near all the wig stores
Should I be in a hotel
in Los Angeles?
Did I miss my plane?

A FEW WORDS ABOUT MYSELF

It was twenty-five to eleven.
I put my hat on.
The boys didn't recognize me.
I'm a real aristocrat.
I went out to dinner,
pot roast and baked potato.
I saw my wife and asked her
for a divorce.
I confessed to the doorman
that he would have to face
the big world out there
without me.
On Tuesday night I got laid.
On Friday I got a haircut.
I picked up a case of beer
on the way home.
I met this punk I hate
on the street and I kicked
his fucking teeth in.
I bought all the papers
and called my consultant.
There was no answer.
I remembered he was
out of town.
I got a new pair of shoes.
I used my new machine,
I waited in the lobby
for my driver.
I had coffee in the study
and read my mail.
Over the weekend I took
my mistress to my hideaway
in the country.

I had all my accounts checked.
I canceled my appointments.
The clerks rearranged my new
furniture. I saw my dealer
and settled our affairs.
The weather took a turn
for the worse. I called
a taxi. I arrived home.
I could still hear this
voice saying to me
kiss me goodbye kiss me
goodbye.

Taking a turn for the worse

When he gets home, he immediately takes off his shoes and socks. Then he changes his clothes. He puts on a flannel shirt and blue jeans, takes them off, puts on brown corduroy pants and a striped polo shirt, no shoes. Takes them off, changes into overalls and work shirt. After dinner, he tries on his expensive suit from Alvin Murray's. Shines his shoes, puts them on. No socks. Finds his watch, puts that on too. Takes everything off again, puts on shorts and a pajama top. He goes to the closet and looks for a hat. He finds the straw hat he got in Woolworth's for a dollar. He puts it on for a while, then takes it off. Switches to his Irish cap from 149th Street and Third Avenue. There's a store there where you can get authentic caps like this. Takes it off, changes to his wool hat, the green one, puts on his army surplus jacket and phys-ed T-shirt and leaves.

When he arrives, he is smiling. All evening he will continue to smile. People say to him "Fuck you!" or "Fuck off!" and he just smiles. He grins and grins. He sings a song and smiles, he takes a piss and smiles, he smiles when he's dancing, he smokes a cigarette and smiles at the same time, he talks and smiles, walks and smiles, drinks and smiles.

He wipes the smile off his face. It gets on his hands. He rubs his hands on his pants and the smile gets on them too. After a while, the smile is all over him. He is very embarrassed at this, so he smiles.

Finally, he decides to leave. He goes to the wrong door, however. Instead of the door he should go to, he heads for the door to the portico. The portico is five stories above the street. He realizes too late, however, that he heading for the door to the portico instead of the right door, but he does not want to spoil his exit, so he smiles.

He steps out onto the portico, but he is still looking back at his audience. He is smiling at them. He realizes too late, however, that the portico is no longer there. Nothing is there, outside the door of the portico. It is a straight drop down five stories. He looks back again at his audience.

The people in the room all begin to smile.

TRIPPING UP THE STAIRS

Near the station under blue skies

the postal clerks unwrap their lunches

and the pretty secretaries unwind

to invisible yoga exercises. I hear

a symphony of muscles relaxing & flick

away my cigarette. I imagine something

poisonous inside me. I care & I don't care.

I buy the Times, Post, and Star

in the drug store & wander into Kramer's.

Executives and lawyers drink cappuccino.

Irish music coming over the speakers.

I listen, surprised. My hangover

is an alien planet of hard edges.

Now the day, opening like a door,

invites me to enter slowly & examine

the cold egg-shaped future.

Living legend

for Jim Brodey

I have no interest in cigars.
Also, no interest in cars.
I took a driving lesson not long ago
and was totally terrified.
I thought it was about time I learned to drive.
But maybe I'm as well off not driving.
There is no place special I want to go.

Cigars make the body more interesting.
But they smell awful.
How things smell is important.
All my friends smell great.
You smell great.

Therefore, you must be my friend.
You were not born again.

I have no real interest in religion
anymore. Except I am interested
in the Archbishop of the Philippines
whose name is Cardinal Sin.

I am not interested in New Jersey.
I am not interested in "the theater."
I am not interested in Prince Charles.

I force myself to stay awake.
I remember that when t.v. screens
were small and black & white,
so was everything else.

APPLAUSE

I am ugly, but I tell you I'm beautiful.

People laugh at my feet. I laugh at
every single part of their bodies.

Ethiopian women are all beautiful.
You are an Ethiopian woman.

Therefore, you are beautiful.
More beautiful than Dominique Sanda

who must also be an Ethiopian woman

because she is so beautiful.

FUGITIVE

for Toby Thompson

I don't want to go to bed anymore.
There are no Yankees. No White Sox.
Late at night, we sing cowboy songs.
I have wood I chew on till I get splinters
in my mouth. Then I go home drunk.

I run to the Safeway, spend $26.
I run to the mailbox. I feel horizontal
and simplified. I zero in. She throws
into question. A car pulls up.
I give the password: treachery.

My complexion has improved. My hair
is thicker. I am more intelligent,
though I have lost the ability
to think abstractly. I go to bed
American, wake up American.

Suddenly I de-materialize.
I am denied form. I still have
a faint orange glow, as do Japanese
mountains. I remember the untimely
way baseball prophecies
flickered in your eyes.

The Them Decade

for Jesse Winch

Hours and hours go by, traffic flows
smoothly through the arteries.
Buses discharge their passengers.

I stand in the middle of the bright day
posing next to the mailbox,
a glum expression on my face.
I wonder what Pete Rose is doing right now.

All I do is drink coffee and smoke.
I want to soak in a tub of ink
and become a masterpiece.
I am tired of the way cab drivers
whine in this city. I love the zone system.

The sun sets as the H-6 cruises
past the World Bank. I wonder
where Robert S. McNamara is right now.

At the Kennedy Center, Fred Astaire
is honored. Ginger Rogers doesn't show up.
Mayor Barry's wife Effi is planning
to host a radio show.
Some people want a white chief of police,
some want a black one. Toby Thompson
flies through Cabin John becoming blonder,
sleeker, crazier. Bernard Welt is always
on the way to teach a class. Doug Lang
remains a mystery. I wonder where
Michael Denney is right now. Somewhere
in Baltimore telling a pointless story
with no end, but brilliant nonetheless.

Now it is dark. I watch the flags
fly on F Street outside the Dubliner.
(Union Station is beautiful at
night.) I long for something permanent.

INFLUENCING THE PAST

I am about to leave. I'm almost out the door.

And balloons of yellow fire fill my head.

There is too much electronic music in my past

which I carry over my shoulder.

I remember too much, I think too much,

I fear too much. I do my sit ups,

my push ups. I practice my Spanish:

cerveza fria, bodega, no fume.

The gravity is ice cold today

and it makes me dizzy. It's drizzling

and I don't want to go. I want to lie

in bed and watch Pancho the Parrot

sing 'I Left My Heart in San Francisco'

on the Johnny Carson Show.

NAKED WALLS

Mornings I am behind curtains
after the cool nuclear dawn

I never touch the floor anymore

I live in

                    the medicine cabinet
                    surrounded

by great medicine

At night I climb down the front of my building
on a rope & go for a midnight swim:
I am trying to be kinder, looser

                    My cat runs away in panic when I approach
                    not even aware of her & that disturbs me

People are always telling me
that they were scared of me when they first met me

Last thing I want to do is spread fear

I keep thinking that not knowing anything
                                        about computers
will be my downfall

My head hurts & I feel more numb than sad
My friend Willie wrote to me & said 'thanks for not dying'
but every day lately I feel like I'm about to let him down

Ted, you look handsome & serious in the picture on the

back cover
of *The Sonnets*, that great book that cut through
to new destinations

I offered you a slug of Irish whiskey last November at St. Mark's
& you gulped some down then you took out
some pills & said to me 'you want a pill?' I said
'what kind of pill?' 'an Irish pill' you told me
I declined
You were great that night

When *So Going Around Cities* came out I told
the editor of the Washington Post book section that
this is the most significant book of poems
of the last 10 or 20 years
but they still didn't review it

I worry about everyone I love
but you were one of those people I didn't worry about
I just figured you'd always be there
like Niagara Falls a natural resource I wish you
hadn't died I wish none of us had to die I don't

want to die so badly it makes me sweat
it makes my eyes hurt it makes my voice
disappear

But at least you died on the Fourth of July:
brilliant, ridiculous, American

what the flatness contains

MYSTERIES

All last night I kept speaking in this

archaic language, because I had been reading

Poe and thinking about him. I read 'The Murders

in the Rue Morgue' which is supposedly the first

detective story. Who dun it? I wondered.

It turns out an orangutan was the murderer.

It looks to me like the detective story got off

to a pretty ridiculous start. I used to visit

Poe's house in the Bronx. I used to think,

God, Poe must have been a midget. Everything

was so small. Poe died in Baltimore and I can see why.

In Baltimore, all the people are very big and sincere.

During dinner last night, I told Doug and Susan

about 'Murders in the Rue Morgue.' I said I hadn't

finished it yet, but it looked like the murderer

was going to turn out to be an orangutan, unless

the plot took a surprising new twist. Then Doug

suggested that he and I collaborate

on a series of detective stories in which

the murderer is *always* an orangutan.

I HATE ETHIOPIAN MUSIC

My house is blue again tonight
as my wife sleeps in the living room
I wish I were innocent! I hate the sound
of moaning from across the street

I have a double NyQuil straight up
Once I sunk into black moods
while altar boys slept by the lake
But now my brother takes me on boat rides
in the dark where menacing figures
refuse to let me piss

I do not like to fuck in taxis
I like to get down on my hands and knees
and watch the angelic mist
drift beyond the horizon

Lapse of Luxury

Here, in a Mexico of doctors, I have feet
and hands, am still alive, am not dead!
I am alive and eating pizza at Vesuvio's
in the marvelous twilight of imperialism
as she waits for a piece of the phone to rub
on her gums. The heat has been turned on.
I can see the harbor from my window
as night falls upon the odor of dark
gray shirts and blue jeans. I am naked
underwater in the black pools of a lake.
I am aware of two very cold cans of Coke
moving up and down my back. I use my elbows
to keep me up. She calls them
"water blisters." I am her "sin-eater."

THE NIHILISTS HAVE NOTHING TO WORRY ABOUT

Something used to happen here,
in the ornamental darkness.

I don't know. Maybe it was
that puppet joke with the string
of your Tampax. Or maybe the way
we clung to the poised extensions
of these orchestral moods.

THE CLEAN SWEEP OF THE STARS

War was declared while rich men in beautiful sweaters
smiled into the camera. I let it all slide.
I own a fortune in clothes.
I see what lies ahead: speed.
I feel my wingless body stall along
the curve. I twitched for a tenth of a millisecond
and everything was different. They told me I would be paid
handsomely and I believed them and said "okay."

And now look at me: they set aside a minute for me
this winter and said over and over: "Show us you can stop.
Show us you can stop."
Speed, they said, and calmness, and fear.

Get swallowed,
they say, it's a nice high: everything seems
to slow down when you are on the inside, renamed,
with no opportunities, delirious, barely moving.

I accelerate, raise the stakes, no one suspecting
I could be so strange.
The plan calls for me to walk to the corner, catch
your eye, apologize, dominate, leave a message—
all with a coolness, a certain unaware dissonance, as though
I were merely an instrument of those beautiful
old rich men. Their pale abundance.

No matter where I go my body stalls along the shift.
The problem is heat. As the speed collects, light
is distorted and in the clarity of my fantasies
I recalculate appearances.

The freer I was, the emptier the sweaters became,
until mountains of old men's shirts begin to drift

toward the rocks, where a gorgeous calmness
could no longer be measured. Vast clouds rose
over me outside the locked bedroom.

THE CLUB SCENE

The sun is a yellow splatter pouring down

on figures that could be mountains or trees

and nearby are fields of brown framed by

two silver borders. There's a boat, a house,

a barge. Everything is clearly distinguishable

but pretty abstract. A young blonde is turning red.

She looks cartoonish, less abstract. It is raining

radios. It is snowing telephone books.

The machine is a small particle of pressure absorbing

the players who sit and brood in a place

that could pass for Kansas, where you can hear someone

practicing the trombone in the hallway. It seems automatic like

a vast police state of "fluids" and "solids." There is one

colossal blue suit. Citizens come here to unfold.

The sun was a blow gun: what it makes, it takes.

The body. A factory. They collapse in America.

There are facial expressions, sofas,

helicopters, cups of coffee. This could be

a "sex test" of victims in ripped T-shirts.

Celebrities seem to turn ugly as they groan

whimpering cries of complete surrender.

Memorial Day

What a strange calamity—
to be stuck here in the light, hot and sweaty!

(The sky falls on my birth.)

I always go to mass in the garden at twilight
where I used to long for hours of atonement in your arms,
but your heart is like a house
and your teeth have eyes!

The elders are sleeping in the doorway,
their arms curled around the doorman,
their women arriving from the valley
dressed in grass skirts, pulling shopping carts.

I am hungry for wickedness, for a knife
and a boat. I have flowers
in my mouth. I have a woman with me
on the road to a foreign land. She is late
and I hear my voice through the myriad voices
of night where my love is pressed against me.

Your sadness is infinite, your voice so vacant,
she says. I am sober, stuck in a tunnel
in my pajamas. I get on my bike.
I am not dead. My face is blank. Girls
in communion dresses kneel in the dust.
My toes touch the ashes in a dream of half-circles.
That's the way we like you, she says.

HAMBURGER GARDENS

The words hang there at breakfast, where crows fly.
You disconnect me in the middle of a conversation
about the wind whistling through your t.v. set.
There's a road that frightens you and that dream
about a box they put you in. You hang me up
and hang me up again. Fur falls like snow.
My animal hisses in the corner of the room.
In a dream about a pink continent
where fur falls like snow
they replace the wind with the hair
on your neck. I sense more corrupt talk
as I strip your clothes off with my teeth.
You light the fingertips of the hands in the audience
and blow on them. The applause starts up again.

The moon

So, this is the moon.
There are only holes
where once there were motels.

But, there *is* a motel somewhere.

Little white men take you to it.

White Reflections

for Tom Raworth

Today was like a Greek ruin, only bigger.

And Greeker. Can you smell that fish?

I smell it everywhere I go these days.

That's why I'm always so solemn.

Accusations make my mouth water.

Oh, that my heart had a nictitating membrane!

I think of sleep as a jamboree.

I think of Marlon Brando as Marlon Brandeaux.

JEWELS

Outside the restaurant I try to remember
the fat boys, the women with vacant stares.
Trembling hands touch the trees. The walls shake
as the breeze blows through your guitar.
I never knew what to eat. I used to hang
over the sink crying. I knew you'd call.
Pieces of cheesecake are served on toothbrushes.
I move the bodies on the stairs away from me,
my friends broken-hearted, my feet cold.
I can't read maps. In the airport I weep again
like an idiot. Bitch, I thought, hide your face
behind the wheel. Now the building rises up
on the corner of the city within the city
where light bulbs are the necklaces of paper boys.

The Love You Take

Next thing I know I'm on my way
to the salon where I peel off my clothes
and my body is arranged by strangers
who, like me, are sweltering and want a cigarette.

These moments collect and settle
throughout the day
until a paralysis of heat overcomes
all ambition and sexual desire
and we are left to our cold supper
in the air conditioned room.

I hear a plane overhead
and a car horn honking below.
My feet and legs hurt.
I am watching the face of the clock.

It is too dangerous to go out.

(The flowers on the bookcase are still alive.)

I am still alive standing in white shorts
on the hill leading to the Hilton
when the day collapses
like a condemned building.

Smoke continues to rise
from my clothes and body.

On the beach

This summer at the seaside
the sand-colored buildings
smelled of Coppertone & somewhere
beyond the boardwalk a transistor
radio was playing Rachmaninoff's Variations
or Rhapsody

or whatever it's called on the theme by Paganini
& you were reminded of that room with the beautiful
chandeliers (dozens of them) in the South of France
& how there were monsters in the room
& we cried & told our Daddies
who said we could sleep out
by the blue pool where the bald man
made eyes at the nubile bathing beauty.

The bald man told us
how much he liked our tiny bodies
& wanted to put us in his pocket
& take us to his house by the bay
to see the fishermen & watch daytime t.v.

We were helpless. We lowered our blankets
to the sand & said "this is it, this is it"
as our feelings of anxiety
ballooned into the red sunset.

with Doug Lang

My EMOTIONS

for Karen Allen

I went to the cafe. I sat down.

We had coffee. I talk only to animals now I told her.

She said she didn't have much money. She rolled my sleeves up.

I said they listen to rock 'n roll. Everybody gets on the floor.

I don't know what love is she said.

I walked very slowly down the corridor.

Our hearts are islands she said. I said yes yes yes.

She said I am standing on a chair smoking a cigarette in color.

I am an old man, I said, on my way to a red airport.

Some waves

Elsewhere, an older man with glasses is staring
at an extremely beautiful young blonde whose eyes
are closed. Her head is tilted back.
Another woman in a blue bikini is chatting
at the poolside with a reclining man in a yellow
bathing suit. A naked woman with wet hair
is clutching an array of towels to her body.
A woman with long tan legs in a wine
colored bathing suit is kneeling in the sand
and bending over backwards, chin up, neck exposed.
A very urbane-looking man in a tuxedo
is out on the terrace for a drink. Two women
huddle under an umbrella. A man plays golf.
Tiny figures hold hands in the extravagant sunshine.

RELIGIOUS ARTICLES

for Diane Ward

We went through the tunnel into the hotel

and watched t.v. in the corridor. Our hair

grew in the subway. I was all in black.

They turned the floodlights on us and we

began repeating ourselves again. I have no desire

to go to India. No desire to go to China.

I am not dying and I'm not embarrassed!

This was the summer of satisfaction,

of silk afternoons when melodramatic girls

sat naked on the kitchen chairs

staring into space waiting for the fabulous

evening to begin. I was defrocked.

Ideas disappeared from my life. Even when

I was sleeping, my hands stayed awake.

Shocking pink and turquoise skies

transformed the mediocrity of the epoch.

When I look back now, I can see that philosophy

washes everything away. I was trembling

as I climbed into the white circle of light

and tasted your taste on my lips

and washed myself in preparation for your welcome.

I flew into your immense words.

You said, “Do you notice how in a certain

light his jet black hair looks blue?”

I lied and said I did.

THE DREAMERS BY THE FOUNTAIN

All the windows were shut and all the blinds down

as I finished my whiskey, curled my lips

and licked the edge of my glass.

I saw the flash of a black animal

in the long damp night and watched the Statue of Liberty

float down the street in front of my building

in my dream. I was behind schedule. I went

up the stairs into the museum and we talked

in strangled little voices. You slipped your empty

glass under the chair and folded your small, neat hands

on the desk. You wouldn't shake my hand. We talked about sex.

The effect was Oriental. I shook my head.

I didn't want to talk about that. We picked up speed.

I looked at the tight-lipped girl. There's no romance

in being alone, you said. I was floating in the air

above the sunlit valley. You held one finger up and grinned.

Those of us stranded in the office

could hear only the stirring of the visitors,

scrubbing their fur among the scattered garments.

Destiny

I'm going to live in a new place. It will
be a sequel to understatement and finally
I'll be happy. It don't take much, folks.
Nope. I mean, people don't owe you happiness.
But that doesn't mean you deserve unhappiness.
I ought to know: once I was so intense
I couldn't get out of bed in the morning.
Once I got so wet, it seemed like nothing
could dry me off. Once I was the voice of attitude.
Not ordinary attitude, but big tough attitude,
attitude so compulsive and precise that light
would grow brighter when I passed by. In traffic,
this was a problem—horrible, fierce *Dont Walk* reds,
the green of *Walk* too good, too inviting, to be true.
But now that's all over. Now I just eat
porkchops and watch the cops go by.

The White Magic of Decay

My legs and hips thicken along the streets

of the capital in June. Flatness made the evening

tumble into the arms of the young white woman

smoking in the Metro station. I try to breathe.

I hear the waiter say how beautiful I am.

Bald men in the hallway dressed in pajamas

are clinging to my tongue. I inhale the spray.

I am alarmed by half-remembered names

from the past. I swallow one. My eyelids

are fat and half-closed, my eyes intoxicated

by the hands of waitresses. I am alone

and overheated. I sit in the empty, dry tub.

Night and day I jabber in my plastic air bubble:

Old Masters, beware of what the flatness contains.

a dream of half circles

Ghosts

In the rain falling on her.
In wide open space I think of.
I wake up without you, smoking
a cigarette, without a moment.
I have no name. The street without looking.

I am awake. I get done in a day.
I try to remember your faults.
The ghosts are covered with footsteps,
without memory, that open like
editions of *Vogue* in the small room
without you where you see everything
without her, without emptiness
without turning to someone in bed.

Les hommes d'aujourd'hui

In my old age I attached myself

to visual sensation:
deserts forests hollow logs

In the empty, dreary room
in his place
I let myself go
never thinking of a single rule

Oh! Here you are in broken tones
where ideas and styles
immerse my body in the most
beautiful green of your shadow

In the picture in the cafe in my opinion
in a museum in my mind
I had been left out of things

A PIECE OF THE ACTION

I flood my eyes/ dusk approaches the American coast
my light moves west/ I'm "on land": spiked hair,
enameled plates, surface information breaking down,
moving around with the aloofness of a stone. Rhapsody.
Edge. Your body. Icebergs (white).
She still finds a way to maintain her amateur.
It all seems big and deep enough to enter.

She could chew her success/ in the big, obvious facts.
She simply follows orders/ the wall, like a second skin,
feast of many strokes. A telephone call from a man
she didn't invent. Opening day. Omnivorous. The beach.
I am looking down from sand and foam. Pre-dawn, out-
burst
of the water, the rock, the sun, the pink, the blue,
the cloud, the sky, the room, the scene.

You dimensionalized me.
Cigarettes:
blocky
tables
and
chairs.

Cleaner, emptier spaces. Distant, gray-lighted. The east
and west ends.

Extremes.
Skyscraper.
The villa.
Trees shrouded in mystery.
Invisible presence.
Waiting for darkness to fall,

he realized his dark side.
Looks familiar,
an unending garden
of rectangles:
cool, withdrawn swimmer
at sea transformed.

THE REBIRTH OF TRAFFIC

The bodies of the nudes twist

in the savage sphere of

moon victims

climax in a distant monument

once you get your teeth

into that sort of reality

you dedicated your linkages

to the weepy night

light & color broke down in a field

(Lyndon Johnson: scaleless)

(Nelson Rockefeller: white ambiguity)

I was a child of the late

night,

the

creamy

membrane

of

edges: no sky is visible

water white hands always becoming

never bathed in air in pleasure but dense like a group of

disturbed fathers

stymied in a tree, absent, continuous, flattening the view

Ashes

White nights into which I empty my heart
of its silver dissolve under the intense
dark lake in the screen I turn to start
with callous green eyes my sense
of the future disappeared one day
in your face bright like chrome
like a touch of sculpture to say
'wake up with an erection' back home
with delicate hands translates to desires
of blue Mediterranean ashes in my white
balance in a monotone already canals of fires
resist me that Sunday in windbreaker light
demolished a monstrous atmosphere in past
flick of your mouth and out of it aghast

Cracks

Your memory devours my diamonds and nerves
reverse your erotic season changes from cold
to accumulate your lovely vacancies my curves
stick in a passionate system to disappear to fold
from the skin in my pocket the chronic street
shining under the favors apologies ambitions
with a giant hug of hours my unfurled feet
vibrated as the gorgeous freeze of conditions
out of the awful thaw of appetite my thirst
for your deserted anarchy gathers the tough
uneasy crusade undifferentiated in the worst
deflation of panic I've ever scored with enough
cracks to radiate in the two thirty despair
of interior fashion tangled in your pubic hair

CERTAIN THINGS HAPPENED

The women are nervous. Telephone reds. Pink legs, wireless.

Remote. Music connected to pain:

Flowers grow out

of your

pool.

Pantyhose in

your mouth.

Your miniskirt floats through the bedroom.

The men are in the dark box.

They stuck together while

you decentralized.

You imitate whatever

she was playing.

I memorized your ear,

your arched fingers,

dramatizing every passing

instinct,

the elegant interval

triggering

incandescent

prairies of delight.

AMNESIA

for Ted Greenwald

Temperature four thousand
degrees below

Frontiers of lovely
black ice

Minutes cracking off

Small things
want to leave

Antique white fashion
the momentum of bliss

Midnight the horizon
cloud of brittle shine